# BACK TO PENTECOST

*Back to Pentecost: Awaking the Church to the Spirit that Launched It*

**Copyright © 2019 by Peter Louis**

All rights reserved solely by the author. The author guarantees all contents are original and do not infringe upon the legal rights of any other person or work. No part of this book may be reproduced in any form without the permission of the author. The views expressed in this book are not necessarily those of the publisher.

Scripture quotations are from the ESV® Bible (The Holy Bible, English Standard Version®), copyright © 2001 by Crossway, a publishing ministry of Good News Publishers. Used by permission. All rights reserved.

**ISBN: 9781704084688**

**LOC Control Number: 2018941576**

*Development by Tall Pine Books*
|| tallpinebooks.com

*Printed in the United States of America

# BACK TO PENTECOST

## AWAKENING THE CHURCH TO THE SPIRIT THAT LAUNCHED IT

PETER LOUIS

BRAVEHEART

DEDICATION

Mom and Dad, I dedicate this book to you. You taught me to follow Jesus and to never ever give up in life, no matter what happens. You both are my heroes. I love you!

Without the Holy Spirit:
God is far away,
Christ stays in the past,
the Gospel is a dead letter,
the Church is simply an organization,
authority a matter of domination,
mission a matter of propaganda,
liturgy no more than an evocation,
Christian living a slave morality.

But with the Holy Spirit:
the cosmos is resurrected and groans
with birth-pangs of the Kingdom,
the risen Christ is there,
the Gospel is the power of life,
the Church shows forth the life of the Trinity,
authority is a liberating service,
mission is a Pentecost,
the liturgy is both memorial and anticipation,
human action is deified.

**—Ignatius di Latakia**
*Discourse given at the Third World Assembly of Churches,*
*July 1968, in The Uppsala Report (Geneva, 1969) 298*

## CONTENTS

| | |
|---|---|
| *Foreword* | xi |
| *Overture* | xv |
| 1. Apollo's Gospel | 1 |
| 2. Paul's Antidote | 7 |
| 3. New Birth and New Nature | 17 |
| 4. Breaking Down the Baptism in the Holy Spirit | 23 |
| 5. Back to the Garden | 37 |
| 6. My Story | 43 |
| 7. Answering Common Misconceptions | 49 |
| 8. An Invitation for More | 59 |
| *About the Author* | 65 |

FOREWORD

God offers to each of us a promise of transforming power. We can receive that power which enables us to deal with all the challenges life brings our way. Pentecost–the power of God in our lives. I am grateful for the circumstances that brought Peter Louis into my home for the first time in India. It was the beginning of a valued friendship. Peter came to teach, share and demonstrate the power of Pentecost.

Peter is a humble, intelligent man who has a heart for God. His prayer for the church is to come into the fullness of Christ through relationship and understand the role of the Holy Spirit to deepen that relationship. Pentecost is an often misunderstood phenomenon in the church. In this new book, Back to Pentecost—Peter sets out to guide us through the word of God in an effort to explore and define the importance of Pentecost and the profound role it has in our daily lives; to bring about transformational change in us and in the church. This book is an honest expression with serious purpose - to see the church come into a bold, broad relationship with God through the Holy Spirit.

Peter and John were both frozen with fear at various points in their relationship to their faith – even to the point of denying Christ outright. However, once filled with the Holy Spirit, they were out preaching the gospel for everyone to hear. In an answer to prayer, fear vanished and with a fresh filling of the Holy Spirit they found the boldness they needed to keep speaking to everyone who would listen about the life-saving Savior that sacrificed His life for our own.

Reading through this outstanding book, I was amazed at the honest, bold, simple way in which Peter delivers this powerful message. This is more than a book of lovely anecdotes. It is a source of divine instruction, demonstrating a path to a fuller, more powerful relationship with Jesus Christ that will transform your life and bring you to a closer relationship with and in God.

Spirit filled living is for every generation. There is a long history throughout the church of ordinary people, of all ages, who did extraordinary things through the power of the Holy Spirit. Every generation has grappled with Pentecost. The tensions across church denominations and the way we interpret and practice Pentecost has always been one of the churches great conversations. Peter has done a great job at keeping this conversation at the forefront of this generation–simply put, Pentecost is for everyone, for every generation.

The Holy Spirit has many functions, roles, and activities in our lives. Peter's book is a generous guide to help us find our purpose in the arms of Jesus, with the Holy Spirit as our guide. There is no doubt that for Peter, writing this book was a labor of love. For you, I hope reading it will be a life changing event.

—**Scott Norling,**
Founder of *Hope Unlimited Church*,
India

OVERTURE

As the church of Jesus Christ, we need a better *explanation* of the gospel and a greater *demonstration* of the gospel. On both fronts, we need something *better* and *greater*. People ask me, what is your ministry about? It's very simple: we carry a heart to *serve* the body of Christ and to deliver the message of God with clarity.

In some camps, we see emphasis on *explanation* while *demonstration* is nullified. In the other ditch, we find attempts at *demonstration* with no accompanying *explanation*. Our heart is to see reconciliation between these two circles, causing harmony and not more discord. Father Raniero Cantalamessa expresses this beautifully in his book Come, Creator Spirit saying, "Whenever Christians allow divisions to separate them, something of their patrimony is fragmented, divided, and lost.

It is as if a mosaic were to end up part in one museum and part in another: no one would any longer have the opportunity to see it and appreciate it as a whole in all its original beauty." I'm submitting this book to you not as a doctrinal line in the sand but as food for thought around a subject that has been hotly contested over the years.

In this book, I wish to unpack the language and revelation that I believe the Lord has given me about where the church is today and what to do about it. The church is not without hidden sin, confusion, and compromise. It's not everywhere... but it's certainly infecting many places.

My heart cry is to see the things that grieve the heart of God be broken off of His bride. I meet so many believers who are full of confusion, depression, and anxiety, and they feel separated from the Father. It's a sad reality, but I believe that God has a message that works as an antidote to these ploys.

*"As the church of Jesus Christ, we need a better explanation of the gospel and a greater demonstration of the gospel."*

Having said that, the *only* antidote we have is found

in the framework of the Word of God. Spirit-oriented believers are often accused of being too experience-focused. It may be a true accusation in certain places; however, the leaders that I found myself being surrounded by are sticklers for the Word of God.

We want to be peacemakers between those who place the majority of their emphasis on the Word and those who place the majority of their emphasis on the Spirit. Part of our ministry is to build a bridge between the Word camp and the Spirit camp.

The well-known British evangelist Smith Wigglesworth once said, "When the Word and the Spirit come together, there will be the biggest movement of the Holy Spirit that the nation, and indeed, the world has ever seen." This is my prayer and hope for you as you read this book, you gain a deeper appreciation and love for the Word of God and the Spirit of God.

On both ends of the spectrum, I've seen stone throwing and attitudes and actions that weren't Christ-like. Word-oriented believers have often dismissed Spirit-oriented believers as loopy flakes who have no concern for doctrine, and likewise, Spirit-oriented Christians have accused Word-oriented Christians of being dry and boring legalists.

Despite all of this, there was a time in history in which both of these camps existed in harmony with one another. Both came together in the gospel mission and the result was an advancement of explanation and demonstration of Christ's saving power. In the following chapters, we'll explore that point in history and how it can benefit our church culture today.

Perhaps you're longing for more. Maybe you've been around the typical "Christian culture" long enough to become calloused to the deeper things of God. Maybe you've been a stone thrower on either side of the doctrinal spectrum. Either way, I pray that the message contained in this book would encourage you to step into a life of fullness in Jesus, totally free from the grip of sin and compromise. Read, and be encouraged to pursue *more*.

> *"The most important fruit of the dialogue between the traditional churches and the Pentecostal churches will be achieving this aim: to recognize that Pentecost does not cast sacrament into a lesser role (especially the sacrament of baptism with water), and neither does sacrament cast Pentecost into a lesser position." (Come Creator Spirit p. 57)*

My wife and I once went on a cruise where we stopped at various exotic locations throughout the Caribbean. On one such stop we attended a little street-side stand where an artist proceeded to draw us in caricature form. If you know anything about a caricature you know that the purpose of the image is to show the various features of the subject in an oversimplified, exaggerated way.

When we received the caricature, the artist had thoughtfully highlighted the "strength" of my nose and the brilliance of my wife's smile. I was obviously not offended at the artists rendition of my nose because there is some truth in "strength" of my nose, as my wife puts it.

In the same way, with my words I would like to sketch a caricature of the face of Traditional Christianity and Pentecostal / Charismatic Christianity. As I seek to sketch these two beautiful expressions of Christianity I mean no disrespect or harm to either expression.

Seeing these faces with their respective features exaggerated may allow us to move beyond our current stagnation and division. For the most part these two camps have unfortunately ceased to dialogue with one another due to offense and disputes that have arisen over doctrinal differences. And the subject of this book, Pentecost and the Baptism of the Holy Spirit, has been at the heart of the division.

Let me make a note that the definitions below of these two expressions of Christianity are not by any means to convey that any one person or church neatly fits into either category. These definitions are an attempt to clearly and concisely give the reader a reference point for where they may be on the spectrum of church belief and practice. These reference points are simply that, a reference point. It is not intended to demean, put down or box in a particular expression of Christianity. I have wrestled to put language to the division that I observe so flagrantly within the Body of Christ because it seems that any attempt at bringing definition only brings greater offense. Proverbs 18:19 illustrates this principle perfectly.

> *"A brother offended is more unyielding than a strong city, and quarreling is like the bars of a castle."*

If I had the chance to speak to the Body of Christ at large, across all denominational and cultural lines, I would share this verse out of Proverbs. We must learn, as believers, to guard ourselves from offense and quarreling over minor differences in our beliefs and the practice of said beliefs.

We must rally, in love and thanksgiving, around what Jesus Christ has done on the cross and the subsequent glories of his death and resurrection. If we are honest, the Body of Christ at large needs to repent of this great folly. We have tolerated offense and quarreling between denominations which has tainted our witness as a whole to the world around us. Perhaps one of the greatest controversies of our day surrounds the subject of Pentecost and the baptism of the Holy Spirit.

Though it is impossible to define the numerable expressions of Christianity, it is my attempt here to speak of what I have seen, experienced and what I know to be true of the traditional church and of the charismatic/pentecostal churches.

I am obviously aware that my perspective is limited to what I have seen and it is my hope that you can receive the following vantage point not as a picture of the whole church but a mere commentary on an issue that has long been wedged between God's precious sons and daughters.

To comment on these things, it is important that we try to define, as best we can, where these two camps exist in their belief and practice of their faith and the primary issues that divide them.

The landscape between the traditionalists and charismatic believers, oversimplified, looks something like this:

The traditional church emphasizes the importance of the Word of God, spiritual discipline such as regularly attending church, having a daily devotional and consistently engaged in discipleship groups. There is also usually a heavy emphasis on overcoming sin through spiritual discipline (Scripture memory, accountability and recovery groups), walking in the light (regularly confessing sin) and eventually sharing your faith with those around you.

Generally speaking traditional church services are somewhat shorter in length than a charismatic or pentecostal church. With the flow of service usually involving one to three worship songs and a 30-45 minute sermon sometimes followed by a short response time. In this sense we see the primary focus of the church is the lead pastor and his exposition of the Word of God.

Traditional churches can be wary of the spiritual gifts such as prophecy, healing and the working of miracles. They caution against an expression of Christianity that seems to rely more on experience and feelings than the truth revealed in the Word of God. Some traditional churches go so far as to say that the gifts of the Holy Spirit have ceased (this group are called cessationists) while other traditional churches may acknowledge that God is able to move in these ways, one can never be sure of his will or certain that he will move in these miraculous ways.

Many traditional churches would also caution someone who claims to hear God's voice citing the only reliable way to know what God is saying is through the Bible. Traditional churches are often accused of being "too religious", "judgmental" or "dry" in their expression of love towards God.

Contrastingly, Charismatic or Pentecostal churches

place a heavy emphasis on experiencing God through the gifts of the Holy Spirit. There is often a strong focus on exuberant praise and worship and extended periods of prayer and fasting.

It is common for individuals in these churches to discuss dreams, visions and prophetic revelation as given by God to lead and guide them and the church.

Generally speaking a charismatic or Pentecostal church service will be longer than a traditional church service with an extended time or worship through song and prayer.

It is not uncommon for the length of the praise and worship time to be the same as the teaching of the Word. The flow of service can often change from week to week depending on the "Spirit's leading" and it would not be abnormal to have a service that lasted three hours.

Believers in charismatic churches are often accused of placing too much emphasis upon their experiences with God. And because of these ecstatic experiences they have also been called out for having an attitude of spiritual pride that has long been off-putting to those who identify with the more traditional expression of Christianity.

However, pentecostal and charismatic believers are rightfully wary of emotionless Christianity that is defined more by a sense of duty and obligation than an attitude of joy and exuberance. The point here is not to argue who is right and wrong. Suffice it to say there is some truth in both camps.

To simplify things even more for the sake of brevity and clarity I would like to submit to you that the traditional church as a whole represents those who have a deep love, respect and honor for the *Word of God*.

While the charismatic and pentecostal church has a deep love, respect and honor for the *Spirit of God*. This is not to say that those in the traditional church do not love the Spirit and that those in the Pentecostal church do not love the Word, that is nonsense. I'm speaking of nuance and emphasis.

One camp focuses more heavily on one than the other. The Spirit and Truth however were never meant to be separate. These two camps to me represent the foundation of a true worshipper of God. As Jesus said, "But the hour is coming, and is now here, when the true worshipers will worship the Father in *spirit* and *truth*, for the Father is seeking such people to worship him." (John 4:23)

Again, these observations are mere generalizations and are not intended to represent these groups as a whole. As I write this I can think of so many different churches that break all of these boxes. For instance I know of a beautiful spirit-filled Anglican church that has married liturgy, sacrament and an expression of the gifts of the Holy Spirit in a way that only our God can do.

So in defining these groups by their extremes I am simply giving you, the reader, handles to come on a journey with me, if I have not already offended you, to re-examine a particular subject that has long divided these two camps.

The subject I would like to talk to you about is *Pentecost*. What happened at Pentecost? Why is it important? What does it mean to baptized in the Holy Spirit? Why is it called the *'promise of the Father'*? How do I know if I am baptized with the Holy Spirit? These questions and many more we will explore in the following pages.

# 1

## APOLLO'S GOSPEL

In order to discover where we are *going*, we've got to be willing to take our own temperature, so to speak, to find out where we *are*. While reading in Acts, I came across a text that I believe is a prophetic picture of our church in America today. The resemblance is uncanny. Not only do we see from the text a *diagnosis* of some of our pitfalls, but *solutions* to get us out of those pitfalls. Let's unpack the characteristics of the beloved Apollos:

> "Now a Jew named Apollos, a native of Alexandria, came to Ephesus. He was an eloquent man, competent in the Scriptures. He had been instructed in the way of the Lord. And being fervent in spirit, he spoke and taught accurately the things concerning

Jesus, though he knew only the baptism of John." (Acts 18:24-25)

Before continuing to read, let's stop and give honor where honor is due. Apollos was an excellent minister and man of God. He was passionate about the things of the Lord and took his teaching seriously. How do we know this? Because of the mentioning of *accuracy* in his teaching. Many teach the Bible, but not all teach it accurately. Despite his accuracy and dedication to the scriptures, the Word places a comma and says, "though he knew only the baptism of John." Let's continue:

"He began to speak boldly in the synagogue, but when Priscilla and Aquila heard him, they took him aside and explained to him the way of God more accurately. And when he wished to cross to Achaia, the brothers encouraged him and wrote to the disciples to welcome him. When he arrived, he greatly helped those who through grace had believed, for he powerfully refuted the Jews in public, showing by the Scriptures that the Christ was Jesus." (Acts 18:26-28)

This is a man whom I believe would be a conference headliner if he were alive today. He knew the Word and spoke with eloquence and boldness. No doubt, he was an amazing individual. Now, the scripture doesn't just honor his excellence, but also points out his ignorance—ignorance not being a harsh word, but a good description for his lack of understanding concerning the place *beyond* John's baptism.

John's baptism was an introductory baptism into the Kingdom. It was an initial expression of forgiveness and repentance. John himself actually said, "I baptize you with water for repentance, but he who is coming after me is mightier than I, whose sandals I am not worthy to carry. He will baptize you with the Holy Spirit and fire." (Matthew 3:11)

Apollos, at this point, hadn't been introduced to that second baptism of Holy Spirit and fire. This was solved by the connection made with Priscilla and Aquila. Something that I so appreciate about this couple Priscilla and Aquila is the fact that they didn't pull Apollos aside to shame or condemn his ministry or to tell him that he was in error and willfully missing out on the deep stuff. No! They simply encourage him and explain the way of God more *accurately.*

They honored Apollos as a man of God. They didn't segregate themselves and say, "Wow, this guy is dry. He doesn't understand the baptism in the Spirit. He can't be in our circle." Apollos didn't feel like he was cut down or belittled. He actually continued his ministry and powerfully refuted the Jews after his encounter with them.

Apollos was already teaching accurately, yet this couple found room for increased accuracy in his ministry. The church was in such an infancy state that factions and divisions weren't yet a consideration. If someone was off in their teaching, separation wasn't an option. Reconciliation and gentle steering was the go-to choice.

It breaks my heart to see people break this biblical model and become condemning instead of encouraging. We cannot guilt people into taking a deeper step with Jesus. We can only love them into it.

I really believe the western church for so long has been under the leadership of Apollos. It's been under the leadership of men and women of God who are amazing, competent in the scriptures, and fervent.

However, the primary thrust of their gospel message has been *the forgiveness of sins*. The crux and focal point of all that they do or teach is forgiveness. It's definitely a worthy topic, but far from the *only* topic.

So many leaders are stuck on John's baptism without jumping into the baptism that John himself actually prophesied about. For example, a famous evangelical Christian leader in our world today talked about how the bottom line of the gospel is our eternity being changed from hell to heaven, and that's it. Now, it's true —that is the most key feature...our salvation! However, it isn't the *only* feature.

*"So many leaders are stuck on John's baptism without jumping into the baptism that John himself actually prophesied about."*

This has nothing to do with one believer being better than another because they have something different than the other. I have utmost respect and honor for those preaching the gospel in this way. I grew up under such teaching, which we will unpack later. I have such a deep desire to honor conservatives while at the same time bridging the relational gap between denominations who have historically broken fellowship over such matters.

It should not be an "us and them" situation. It's about *all* believers experiencing everything that Jesus died to give them. But until we are willing to humble ourselves and acknowledge that there is room to grow in the area of Christ-likeness, we will stay divided.

Despite conflicting ideas in church culture today, I believe it is possible to see opposing groups reconciled within the church. It requires receptive hearts and humble spirits on both sides. It isn't about "fixing" the other party. It's about inviting the church into a deeper encounter with God.

We aren't selling a doctrine or peddling a theology; we are simply making available the same Holy Spirit encounter that permeates the book of Acts.

## 2

## PAUL'S ANTIDOTE

IMMEDIATELY AFTER APOLLOS RECEIVED ENCOURAGEMENT from the apostolic couple Priscilla and Aquila, Paul began to make his way into the region where Apollos had been teaching and making disciples at Ephesus. Apollos was seeing conversions. Folks were coming to Christ. Any harvest is a good harvest; however, he had been teaching with a limited revelation. This *lack* manifested when Paul approached some disciples in the area.

> "And he said to them, 'Did you receive the Holy Spirit when you believed?' And they said, 'No, we have not even heard that there is a Holy Spirit.' And he said, 'Into what then were you baptized?' They said, 'Into John's baptism.'" (Acts 19:2-3)

Now, it's key to note that he was speaking to believers. How do we know? Because verse one said, "there he found some disciples" and verse two says, "when you *believed*." These disciples clearly didn't seem offended by Paul's tone. We can bet that he wasn't talking down to them or belittling them with the question. It wasn't Paul's chance to show off his knowledge and expose someone else's lack of knowledge. He genuinely wanted to pour out what he had! The reason that they hadn't heard that there was a Holy Spirit is because the teacher who converted them (Apollos) also didn't have such understanding! Everything flows from the top down. Paul continues his conversation:

> "And Paul said, 'John baptized with the baptism of repentance, telling the people to believe in the one who was to come after him, that is, Jesus.' On hearing this, they were baptized in the name of the Lord Jesus. And when Paul had laid his hands on them, the Holy Spirit came on them, and they began speaking in tongues and prophesying." (Acts 19:4-6)

This is so profound. Priscilla and Aquila were *explaining* the gospel more clearly, then Paul came *demonstrating* the gospel more clearly. Paul wasn't trying to create a new camp or denomination here by adding to Apollos' teachings. He came to provide an *experience* along with the teaching. He came to make room for more than the baptism of John. He came to make room for the baptism in the Holy Spirit. Let's not forget, when Paul posed his question, he was not merely referring to the *knowledge* of the Holy Spirit in a general sense, but was referring to the *baptism* in the Holy Spirit in a specific sense.

Had he been referring to the Holy Spirit in general, he would have said something like, "Hey folks, the Holy Spirit indwelled you when you were saved. That's as much as you get." No! He came to give the knowledge of the actual baptism in the Spirit and not just an introduction to the Person of the Spirit.

As a pastor for the last seven years I have met so many people who are certain of their salvation, but are unsure whether or not they have been baptized into the Holy Spirit. This confusion in these believers is evidence to me that we have been under the leadership of Apollos. Again, I do not say this as a condemnation, but to make the point that many Christians are confused about the baptism of the Holy Spirit because those who led us to Christ were uncertain as well.

I'd like to make a note, it would be a mistake for us, as a people, to avoid the baptism in the Spirit because people in the past have misused it or abused it. That's like avoiding the Word of God because people have misused the Word of God. Paul wasn't concerned about being misread or misunderstood. He simply came to bring a revelation of the heart of the Father. He wasn't hindered or hesitant because of the potential of being misunderstood.

> *"It would be a mistake for us, as a people, to avoid the baptism in the Spirit because people in the past have misused it or abused it."*

I truly believe that this is what the baptism of the Holy Spirit is: it's a revelation of the heart of God. It's an antidote to stale, surface level Christianity. It is the fulfillment of everything that Jesus provided on the cross. The Bible describes this experience as the "Promise of the Father" (see Acts 2:39). Why wouldn't we want to experience something with such a sacred description?

## A SUBSEQUENT EXPERIENCE

> "But when they believed Philip as he preached good news about the kingdom of God and the name of Jesus Christ, they were baptized, both men and women. Even Simon himself believed, and after being baptized he continued with Philip. And seeing signs and great miracles performed, he was amazed.

Now when the apostles at Jerusalem heard that Samaria had received the word of God, they sent to them Peter and John, who came down and prayed for them that they might receive the Holy Spirit, for he had not yet fallen on any of them, but they had only been baptized in the name of the Lord Jesus. Then they laid their hands on them and they received the Holy Spirit." (Acts 8:12-17)

"The experience is distinct from that of regeneration. Of those Samaritans who had believed and been baptized in the name of the Lord Jesus it was said that they had not yet been baptized of the Holy Ghost. It is evident, therefore, that a man may be born again of the Spirit and not be baptized with the Spirit. In regeneration there is a gift of life by the Spirit, and whosoever receives it is saved; in the Baptism of the Spirit there is a gift of power, and by it the believer is equipped for service and endued for witnessing." —**Samuel Chadwick**, The Way of Pentecost 1932

Chadwick puts great language to the heart of God concerning these things. The fullness of the Spirit (or the grace of God) wasn't fully given and released at the moment of salvation. It is not to say that it always happens this way but this is especially the case for those who have come to Christ without hearing about the baptism of the Holy Spirit.

If faith comes by hearing, and hearing the word of God, how can the hearers believe in the baptism of the Holy Spirit if all that is preached to them is the forgiveness of sins and a passport to heaven? It is clear then that the generation of believers who have come to faith through the "Apollos of our day" were unable to enter into this promise of the Father because the Word was not preached to them.

As the larger Gospel-picture unfolds we see that salvation was a means of bringing the world out of sin but that the baptism of the Holy Spirit is about putting God back into man. In the same way God rescued Israel from Egypt to bring them into the Promised Land, so he delivers us from sin to bring us into His very presence.

In the instance of those who came to faith without the understanding or invitation of the baptism of the Holy Spirit, it must be a subsequent experience to their initial moment of salvation.

Some find it hard to wrap their minds around the reality that such a valuable experience wouldn't be given by default at salvation. This baptism isn't given by default at our conversion, but it is made available at salvation to those who ask.

We see a similar pattern in the Old Testament that will help illustrate this truth. When God delivered Israel from Egypt (which represents our slavery to sin) their salvation and journey with God was not complete. In fact the joy that they experienced on the other side of the Red Sea would pale in comparison to what God intended to give to them in the way of a land flowing with milk and honey. We know that that generation failed to enter into the Promised Land because they doubted in the promises of God and put him to test by their rebellion and complaining.

In the same way, I think many believers have experienced a Red Sea moment with God. They have been delivered from a life of sin and death by putting their faith in the death, burial and resurrection of Jesus.

However they have yet to receive the "promise of the Father" (the baptism of the Spirit) that was intended to accompany those who were saved. Thankfully for us, we do not have to displace people to receive our promise, we simply have to ask!

Jesus said, "If you then, who are evil, know how to give good gifts to your children, how much more will the heavenly Father give the Holy Spirit to those who ask him!" (Luke 11:13)

> *"This baptism isn't given by default at salvation, but it is made available at salvation to those who ask."*

The scriptures display this divine sequence clearly. It

is important to note that this divine sequence is not a formula or necessarily the *only* way in which someone receives the baptism of the Holy Spirit, but it does reveal something to us about the heart of the Father.

God intended to cleanse the temple before He filled it. We can see great intention and purpose in our Father as we study this sequence of events. Now, can people experience the baptism of the Spirit at the moment of salvation? Absolutely. However, we would know when such an event takes place and if we don't know, we have biblical permission to pursue the second experience of the baptism on the Spirit.

In the text we are about to read, Jesus had been crucified and raised from the dead, and His blood was to be put on the mercy seat; from that position of completion, He appeared to His disciples.

Up until now, they were followers of Jesus, but hadn't experienced true regeneration because the plan of redemption hadn't been carried out through His sacrifice. Christ appears to them toward the end of the gospel of John:

> "And when he had said this, he breathed on them and said to them, 'Receive the Holy Spirit.'" (John 20:22)

This was the disciples' born-again experience. As

God breathed into Adam and he became a living creature, so Christ breathes into his disciples and they become new creations! This was the Holy Spirit being breathed into them, as He is for *every* new convert. It was 50 days later that they were baptized in the Holy Spirit on the day of Pentecost.

If this John 20 experience was the only Holy Ghost encounter that the disciples needed, Christ would have skipped the upper room experience in Acts 2 and simply sent them out. In this case there was a separate encounter with the Person of the Holy Spirit that came after the disciples were born again.

## 3

## NEW BIRTH AND NEW NATURE

THE BAPTISM IN THE HOLY SPIRIT IS GOD *LONGING* TO become so close with us that He actually clothes us with Himself. See, Christ dying and raising up was a move to prepare us to be recipients of the Holy Spirit. The blood cleansed our hearts from every ounce of sin.

> "For it is impossible for the blood of bulls and goats to take away sins. Consequently, when Christ came into the world, he said, 'Sacrifices and offerings you have not desired, but a body have you prepared for me…'" (Hebrews 10:4-5) John also relates, "Behold, the Lamb of God, who takes away the sin of the world!" (John 1:29)

John's proclamation was not just the *forgiveness* of

sin, but the *removal* of sin. In our Christian life, we can easily attempt to limit the blood of Christ to the blood of bulls and goats. What do I mean by that? People all over the church world get forgiven, they sin, then they keep coming back to Christ for the forgiveness of sins like in the Old Covenant.

In the Old Covenant, a priest would slaughter an animal to atone for sin, the people would leave, continue in sin with no heart change, and then return to the priest for forgiveness. Under the Old Covenant, there was atonement for *sin,* but not freedom from *sinfulness*. If we aren't careful, we'll receive forgiveness and then leave Christ's presence with zero change, only to return later with a guilty conscience from the same habitual sin.

I want to see believers set free from the grip of sin and walk in the fruit and gifts of the Spirit to see the world reconciled to God through love.

## THE MISGUIDED CONCLUSION

The inferiority of the Old Covenant was an inability to remove the inward propensity for sin because of an insufficient sacrifice. Now that a sufficient sacrifice has been made, our flesh can and *will* be subdued for those who put their trust in Christ. I really believe that so much of our modern teaching has been flawed because we are teaching people that their nature is still sinful, and as a result, sinful living follows.

Here is the conclusion that we jump to: if I still sin, then it must be because I still have a sinful nature. The problem with that thinking is that it's an Old Covenant mindset. It's a law-minded way of viewing God. It's an approach to God that gives you confidence if you've been good and strips you of your confidence if you've been bad.

It was all external and performance based. The beauty of Jesus is that His New Covenant invites us into a relationship with God that isn't based on our works, but His grace.

Paul relates, "For sin will have no dominion over you..." Why? Because of the second half of the verse: "since you are not under law but under grace" (Romans 6:14).

The idea that we still have a sinful nature contradicts the very blessing that Jesus brought us into. The scriptures are littered with language regarding newness and oneness:

> "But he who is joined to the Lord becomes one spirit with him... Or do you not know that your body is a temple of the Holy Spirit within you, whom you have from God? You are not your own..." (1 Corinthians 6:17-19)

"By which he has granted to us his precious and very great promises, so that through them you may become partakers of the divine nature." (2 Peter 1:4)

"Therefore, if anyone is in Christ, he is a new creation. The old has passed away; behold, the new has come." (2 Corinthians 5:17)

What is the point of a new birth if we still have an old nature? How can someone who has literally been born of God still be a mere *sinner*? How can a sinful nature of sin not vanish when the blood of Jesus is applied? To think that a sinful nature remains is to assume that the blood of Christ is insufficient.

The gospel gives us permission to consider ourselves dead to a sinful nature and alive to all that is holy. Georgian Banov said, "If we are only free from sin when we die, then Jesus isn't our Savior... death is." A common Christian catchphrase that's unfortunately found in the church is, "Well, I am just a sinner saved by grace." No! You're not a sinner any longer! You have a born again nature. It might be buried under piles of repetitive sin and unrighteous thoughts and feelings.

However, at your core is a new nature in Christ! Saying that you are not a saint because you struggle with sin is like saying a baby is not a human because it can't walk. Don't judge yourself for where you are, but who you've been made to be. Let the true gospel tutor you, not your sinful experience! All too often we become deceived by our own sinful experience in the Christian life. We become impressed with our ability to sin, and as a result, it steals our focus. All along, Christ has been awaiting our gaze to empower us to live free!

We now have the ability to live and walk in and by the Spirit of God. Galatians 5:16 declares, "But I say, walk by the Spirit, and you will not gratify the desires of the flesh." You might wonder, what does this new nature and righteous living have to do with the Pentecost? Simple! Without an understanding and experience with the Holy Spirit and His baptism, gratification of the flesh and old nature thinking become readily available.

In my first book, *Back to the Gospel*, I exhaust this topic in great detail. It's time to keep our minds renewed to the new nature that has come. In so doing, we'll live accordingly.

The baptism in the Holy Spirit isn't merely the exciting display of miracles, gifts, prophecy, and healings. In fact, you can operate in the gifts of the Holy Spirit without having the fruit of the Holy Spirit. That's a dangerous place to be.

The baptism in the Holy Spirit is *empowerment* to walk in the DNA of Christ. One of the greatest miracles that the baptism in the Spirit provides is a newfound ability to live out your God-given identity.

> *"You can operate in the gifts of the Holy Spirit without having the fruit of the Holy Spirit. That's a dangerous place to be."*

An inner life with God produces the fruit of the Spirit automatically. It's like a chain reaction. Our lives will look more like Jesus with a revelation of the Spirit's empowerment.

Don't allow yourself to be stuck in the mire of Old Covenant thinking. Renew your mind to the new nature and embrace the Spirit's help. Remember and thank God that a sacrifice has been made that has cleaned up and cleared out the altar of your heart to be a landing pad for the presence of God.

# 4

## BREAKING DOWN THE BAPTISM IN THE HOLY SPIRIT

FEAR, PRIDE, CONFUSION, AND CONTROVERSY OFTEN surround the unique topic of the baptism of the Holy Spirit. Much of the controversy has come from advocates of the baptism, in fact.

Some years ago, a group of Pentecostals began to say that if someone doesn't speak in tongues then they don't have the Holy Spirit. Obviously, it was an incorrect conclusion that caused much division. Paul said, "Do all speak in tongues?" (1 Corinthians 12:30) The obvious answer being, no. However, they began making these rules that were unscriptural concerning God's blessing.

John Piper released a great article a while back in which he talked about how there are four references in the book of Acts in which people receive the baptism in the Holy Spirit and speak in tongues. However, there are nine accounts of people not receiving tongues as a two-step process at conversion. I write all of that to say that we need to agree that the gift of tongues doesn't *always* accompany the baptism in the Holy Spirit, but it does *sometimes* accompany the baptism in the Spirit.

I also want to mention that one of the issues I see is a mindset that declares the baptism in the Spirit is only available to the spiritually mature who have jumped through the proper hoops and have completed the proper spiritual disciplines to qualify themselves for the gift.

This mentality says that the baptism is a token of God's blessing on the mature as a reward for running the race well. I contend with this on the basis that the believers in Acts 1 who were baptized in the Spirit had only been reborn for 50 days. As we talked about earlier, their born again experience happened in John 20, post-resurrection, just a short time earlier. This gift isn't reserved for the mature; it's reserved for those who *ask*.

A few years ago my friend Wade and I had the privilege of meeting the great German Evangelist Reinhard Bonnke. In 1974, Evangelist Bonnke founded Christ for All Nations (CFAN) and in the years since its formation his ministry has seen over 78 million people make decisions to follow Christ through many large Gospel crusades held mainly on the continent of Africa. After hearing Evangelism Bonnke speak, at the age of 76, it was clear to us that this man was on fire for Jesus. He spoke with such clarity and passion for people to know the love of Jesus and the urgency to make Him known.

Being so moved by his passion, zeal and longevity we decided to approach him and ask him the secret of his burning heart. My friend Wade approached and asked, "Mr. Bonnke, you are still on fire for God after all these years, how have you kept the fire burning all this time?" Bonnke chuckled and replied with his deep German accent, "Keep the fire burning? Keep the fire burning? I was baptized with the Holy Spirit when I was ten years old and it IS THAT FIRE, the FIRE of the HOLY SPIRIT that has KEPT ME BURNING all these years."

Perhaps the greatest evangelist the world has ever seen credits his longevity, fruitfulness in ministry and passion to an encounter with the Holy Spirit he had at age 10 (now 78) whereby he received a fire that has preserved and sustained him throughout 30 plus years of ministry to the nations. It is clear from this testimony that God did not wait to bless our dear brother Reinhard with the Holy Spirit AFTER he proved himself a faithful man of God.

For years it has been taught in more traditional churches that there is no difference between "receiving the Holy Spirit" at the moment of salvation and the baptism of the Holy Spirit. This belief has unfortunately left a lot of people lacking who do not understand the difference between the work of the Holy Spirit that regenerates us and the work of the Holy Spirit that empowers us to live the Christian life. Biblically these are two distinct works:

## 1) THE REGENERATING WORK OF THE HOLY SPIRIT

Titus 3:5, "He saved us, not because of works done by us in righteousness, but according to His own mercy, by the washing of regeneration and renewal of the Holy Spirit."

This verse of course referencing the work of the Spirit at the moment of our rebirth, to cleanse us from sin and cause us to be born again into a covenant relationship with God through His Son Jesus Christ. The way we know we have been washed clean by the Holy Spirit is that we have confidence that our sins are forgiven, we have peace with God and we are certain that we will live with him forever in heaven.

We have a desire to please God, to walk in His ways and to make Him known. This is all evidence of a life that has responded to the work of Jesus on the cross and been washed and born again by the Holy Spirit. However in addition to this promise of cleansing and regeneration (what most people call their moment of salvation) we were also, through the Gospel, promised power.

## 2) THE POWER OF THE HOLY SPIRIT

> Acts 1:8, "But you will receive power when the Holy Spirit has come upon you, and you will be My witnesses in Jerusalem and in all Judea and Samaria, and to the end of the earth."

This verse clearly references a point in time whereby the disciples would receive a supernatural power, the power of God in the form of the Holy Spirit, which would enable them to be witnesses to the fact that Jesus is alive. The way we know we have been baptized in the Spirit and have received this power from God is a life that is marked by a supernatural power. Power to walk righteously, resisting the temptations and desires of the flesh. Power to make Jesus known through word and deed. Power to overcome disappointment, rejection and persecution.

I meet countless believers who were taught extensively of the first work of the Holy Spirit (the work of regeneration) yet were never instructed in the baptism of the Holy Spirit. It becomes clear then that those believers who were taught that the work of regeneration and the baptism of the Spirit are one and the same have a lot of confusion and fear around this subject.

The fear is that if they do not have the baptism of the Spirit they are not saved. This is absurd. There are countless believers that I have met over the years who love God, are grateful for what he has done yet feel powerless against the lust of the flesh and subsequently feel powerless to make Jesus known.

As we referenced earlier, we this same sequence take place in Acts 8, where Philip is preaching in Samaria with signs and wonders. Masses are baptized into Jesus and saved. It wasn't until later that Peter and John showed up and laid hands on them to receive the secondary experience of the baptism of the Spirit.

I'm not saying that the baptism in the Holy Ghost is *always* a secondary experience. I do believe that often regeneration and the baptism in the Holy Ghost occur simultaneously.

There is much fear among conservatives around this topic. The concern is that it's dangerous placing too much emphasis on *experience* with God instead of the *Word* of God because we can get deceived by our experience.

It's a completely valid concern. However, if our walk with God is void of experience, then we aren't walking with God, we are walking with doctrine. When you look at the Bible, you cannot find a single person who walked with God who didn't experience God. The Bible gives us permission to experience Him.

*"If our walk with God is void of experience, then we aren't walking with God, we are walking with doctrine.*

## HOW DO I KNOW?

I talk to believers who say, "I really don't know if I got baptized in the Spirit when I was saved." The best way to navigate this question is to break down practically what this experience is.

Jesus said, "And behold, I am sending the promise of my Father upon you. But stay in the city until you are clothed with power from on high" (Luke 24:49). Then again in Acts, He stated, "But you will receive power when the Holy Spirit has come upon you, and you will be my witnesses in Jerusalem and in all Judea and Samaria, and to the end of the earth" (Acts 1:8).

This experience is a very *real* moment. It's an event. When you were water-baptized, you can point to the exact moment and place in which it happened. You can recall the place and time... it's unforgettable in many ways. Likewise, with the baptism in the Spirit, it would be strange to say that we've been baptized in the Holy Spirit without knowing when or where it happened.

Perhaps you received this power the moment you were born again and instantly you not only felt forgiven and accepted but you felt empowered by God to walk just like Jesus. But perhaps you feel like you are still missing something.

But regardless of where you think you are, the litmus test for the believer and the evidence of the baptism of the Holy Spirit is the power of God in their life. When I say power I do not just mean an outward display of miraculous gifts (though this is likely), but also the *fruit* of the Spirit.

The power of the Spirit produces the fruit of the Spirit. We know that we have been baptized in the Holy Spirit because there is a grace and power at work within us producing the attitude and character of Christ.

*"The power of the Spirit produces the fruit of the Spirit."*

When you're baptized into Christ, you come out with a new nature. Everything is changed! When you are baptized in the Spirit, you come up clothed with an endowment of power that wasn't there before. A power to know God more intimately, to praise Him more passionately and to make him known more effectively. You gain a boldness to witness and an unashamed approach to the public display of the gospel. It becomes undeniable. In fact, this radical experience produced many of the bold early-church martyrs that we read about.

This teaching isn't to create "haves" and "have nots" within the church. It isn't to point to Spirit-baptized believers as superior or somehow higher ranking. Remember, in Acts 19, the believers whom Paul encountered didn't feel inferior. They simply opened themselves to what they lacked. For a lot of us, the baptism of the Spirit is viewed as an extracurricular encounter that's just a fringe benefit of being a Spirit-camp Christian.

I believe much of this reasoning has come from teachers and preachers boiling the gospel down to a mere ticket to heaven. We have substituted an *eventual* leap into heaven for the necessary element of the baptism in the Spirit that Jesus Himself emphasized to the church. The baptism in the Holy Spirit is not an afterthought of the gospel, but the climax of the gospel. It's the distinguishing factor of Christianity. The infilling and overflowing of God's Spirit in mankind separates this faith from any other.

This baptism is a promise from our Father in heaven

that Jesus fulfills by joining His people to a true intimacy with the Holy Spirit. This is an experience that we can't afford to miss. Any believer from any denomination values *experience*. Consider this: in a relationship, you value experience. If you aren't experiencing a person, that connection with them will be pretty stale.

Encounters, experiences, and real moments together make relationship rich and exciting. Yet somehow we come into relationship with God and it's supposed to be doctrine and precepts on paper with no experience at all. We've been taught to be ultra-cautious with experience with God. There is some truth to that. We must be balanced in our approach and not base our entire life on experience. However, we will miss out if we write off experience all together and live outside of the enjoyment of God-encounters.

My desire is that this teaching would *provoke* you without needlessly *offending* you. I want to show where we are called without condemning anyone for where they are not. In the same way that we came out of the waters of baptism completely wet, I want to see a company of people come out of the baptism in the Spirit soaked and saturated with God Himself.

> *"My desire is that this teaching would provoke you without needlessly offending you."*

## JOHN'S BAPTISM AND JESUS' BAPTISM

When John the Baptist was baptizing people in the Jordan river, all of Israel was coming out to be baptized in water. People were showing up, repenting of sin, and being forgiven in water baptism. It's the reason why Jesus described John as the greatest prophet. His ministry offered the forgiveness of sins without an immediate blood sacrifice. If you know anything about Old Covenant redemption, you know that this was unprecedented. Back then, if you wanted any sort of atonement or remission of sin, blood sacrifice was a must. To be able to offer this without blood was unheard of.

Herein lies the main difference between John's baptism and Jesus' baptism: those baptized by John were presenting themselves in their sin. Those baptized by Jesus were presenting themselves in their righteousness which was given to them as a gift (see Romans 5:17).

The disciples in the upper room were completely cleansed of their sin and pure in heart because of the blood of the Lamb. God had a blank canvas of hearts in the upper room that He could fill. The blood of Christ at the cross cleansed the temple; Pentecost filled the temple.

John's water-baptism took in the sinner and made

them outwardly clean. The baptism of Holy Spirit and fire takes in those who are clean and makes them empowered and dangerous to the kingdom of darkness.

The cross is the greatest expression of love the world has ever seen, but the story of redemption doesn't stop there. It's the first, of a three-fold promise of redemption. God promised the Messiah, who was revealed in all His glory on the cross. But He also promised the Holy Spirit to those who would accept the Messiah as their personal Savior.

Finally, He promises us that Christ will one day return and save those who are eagerly waiting for Him. Redemption was initiated as the cross, sustained by Pentecost and will be completely fulfilled at His glorious return!

The cross was a preparatory plan of redemption, making room for us to be filled and flooded with God Himself. When your slate is clean and clear through regeneration, you qualify for this experience. It isn't weird, odd, or mystical. It's simply reaching out by faith, asking and receiving the baptism in the Holy Spirit. It requires a distinct humility to understand that we not only need sin forgiven, but our temple filled with all that God has.

People often wonder, who baptizes us in the Holy Spirit? John the Baptist gave us the answer: "He (Jesus) will baptize you with the Holy Spirit and fire" (Matthew

3:11 emphasis added). Jesus is the baptizer. It isn't the person laying hands on the other. It isn't we ourselves. It isn't anyone or anything but Jesus Christ Himself baptizing us in the Spirit and empowering us to know him and to make him known.

## 5

## BACK TO THE GARDEN

I'M AFRAID THAT IN THIS DAY AND AGE, WE'VE SETTLED for an expression of Christianity that doesn't reflect what we read in the Book. It's a problem, because the world now sees the hypocrisy of the church because we as a people are trying to live out a Christian label without a genuine experience with the living God. As we read earlier, the baptism is the "Promise of the Father."

It's not "a promise of the Father" but "*the* Promise of the Father." It isn't just another promise that God throws out on the dinner table for His kids. It's a central promise to the functioning of God in our lives.

Allow your heart to grab these things. Let your spirit *experience* the ordained promises. The Lord's promises are all *experiential*. For example, I had a cup of coffee this morning. I experienced it. I didn't read about coffee or study coffee. I didn't go around telling everyone what coffee might be like. I actually drank it and experienced it for myself. If we aren't experiencing God, we are missing out on all that God has for us. If we are only telling people about Him without meeting with Him, we've placed ministry and orating above the encounter-based life we were meant for.

"But we have this treasure in jars of clay, to show that the surpassing power belongs to God and not to us." (2 Corinthians 4:7) Another translation says we have treasure in earthen vessels. As people, we carry treasure within us. Many people have had hands laid on them and experienced the healing touch and power of God through the treasure that was in that minister of God. We ought to not only believe for, but hunger and yearn for experience with God.

It was the Father's desire to regain what was lost in the garden, which is complete intimacy with humanity. His heart's longing was not satisfied until this took place. God's desire for intimacy with man wasn't fulfilled at Christ's resurrection. It was fulfilled at Pentecost when His Promise was poured out and He clothed humanity with Himself. The completion of the threefold promise, however, will be complete when Jesus returns for His bride in glory. As each of these promises are fulfilled, the Father is closer and closer to the ultimate prize of us being with Him forever!

> *"It was the Father's desire to regain what was lost in the garden, which is complete intimacy with humanity. His heart's longing was not satisfied until this took place."*

The baptism in the Holy Spirit reveals such oneness and intimacy. It is core to carrying out our commission to win souls and advance the Kingdom. If you heard a gospel that didn't give you permission to walk and think and act like Jesus...you didn't fully hear the gospel.

Listen, there are plenty of religions that promise life after death, as does Christianity. Our distinction as a faith isn't life after death. The distinguishing marker of Christianity is that Christ literally takes His people and dips them into His own Spirit, empowering them to reproduce the character of Christ on the earth! Highlighting these distinctions causes the church and God's fullness to become attractive. We will never shame anyone into walking this out. We can't beat people up or argue them into fullness. Simply presenting what's available in love is the solution.

> "So faith comes from hearing, and hearing through the word of Christ." (Romans 10:17)

The gospel that I heard growing up actually didn't even give me the faith to believe that I could be filled with God's Spirit. Your Christian experience or lack of it comes directly from the Word of God. We aren't seeking extra-biblical encounters, but biblical encounters that are found within the framework of the Bible.

The struggle we find ourselves in is knowing the standards of the Bible, but not having the fuel we need to actually adhere to those standards. If that is you, you probably find yourself camping out in Romans 7. You do the things that you don't want to do and you don't want to do the things that you know you ought to do! The struggle is real when we find ourselves knowing the truth without applying the truth. The touch of God that we've been unpacking is the fuel in our tank. It's the lift we need to reign above sin and the flesh.

The difference between wanting to do right and our inability to do right is the place where guilt, shame, and condemnation are born. I experienced this badly over a 7 year period and the shame was cancerous to my spirit. It's absolute torment. I've had friends who have literally taken their own lives because of the agony of wanting to do right but feeling powerless to do so. This is a tragedy that the baptism in the Holy Spirit came to redeem!

Being baptized in the Spirit isn't a flaky charismatic phenomena. It isn't a rally of odd-ball believers gathering around, making up prophecies. It's the literal, absolute power of God causing people to be free in every way on every level of their lives. It's an encounter that energizes us to live beyond ourselves and lay down our lives for the bold furtherance of the Word of God. It's God Himself bringing us back to the intimacy that Adam had in the garden before the fall. The plan of redemption is to dip saints into the Spirit of God to go out and reproduce themselves in a world who desperately needs it.

# 6

## MY STORY

I was born again when I was 4 years old. We were in New Jersey, and at night, my mom was sharing the gospel with my brother. She explained that Jesus came to die for our sins so that we could receive Him and live in eternal relationship with Him and go to heaven one day when we pass on if we acknowledge that He is Lord. It was beautiful, and as she shared, my heart was provoked and I prayed the prayer and gave my heart to Jesus.

From that moment on, I knew Jesus and the forgiveness of sins. As much as a 4 year old can, I lived for Jesus. As I grew up, I adopted my parents' faith and started exploring the Bible, going to church, and so forth. I knew that I was forgiven, but had no real understanding of the Holy Spirit and the power of God.

As I mentioned, the disciples in Acts 19 at Ephesus were saved, but had no concept of the functional role of the Holy Spirit. I personally empathize with these believers because I grew up with the same mentality. I grew up with a void in my understanding. In my mind, the Trinity was God the Father, the Son Jesus, and the Word of God. I may have heard token phrases about the Holy Spirit living in me, but it wasn't a daily reality by any means.

Somewhere along the way, I felt myself being ensnared into lust by the enemy. On the outside, I was the "good Christian kid," but on the inside, I had a deep struggle with pornography. I wasn't a partier; in fact, I was afraid of public sin and that whole lifestyle. However, privately, I was so gripped by this addiction. I remember crying out to God, desperately wanting to be free. I would say, "God, I know that You are powerful, but if You're so powerful, why am I so addicted to this?" I was riddled with guilt, shame, and condemnation.

I actually remember being at a group church meeting when I was in the seventh grade and one of my friends asked if masturbation was something that men would always struggle with. The leader was a married man and a spiritual man whom I looked up to very much and he said, "Yes, it's a fight that we will always struggle with." In that moment, I actually began to believe the lie that it was impossible to live free from sin.

From that moment on, anytime I was tempted, I would hear that leader's voice say, "Yeah, it's just something that men will always struggle with." It provided me with an easy way to cave in those moments, because, after all, even the spiritual leaders will never be free from it.

Reproducing these sorts of strongholds as leaders can actually cause those who listen to you to become concreted in sin.

Often in the name of "sympathizing with weakness," we actually provide an easy excuse for remaining in sin. Jesus is interested in raising the standard, not lowering it.

I finally came to a broken place in college. I began to cry out to God desperately. I had been provoked by a recent message that I had heard about breaking the cycles of sin and *staying* free. The speaker talked about not continually returning to the altar to get forgiven of repetitive sin, but actually eliminating the needless cycle all together.

In my spirit, I cried out to the Lord and said, "I know You're powerful and Your Word declares that I am free, but it's not my experience and it's not my reality!" I began to press into God and I actually became angry and honest with God. I said, "Lord, I am not going to let this struggle keep me from You. If You can't handle me with my sin, then I need a different god."

I hated the sin that I was living in. You've got to learn to get *real* with God. He is okay with that... read the Psalms. It took me years, but I finally opened my heart and asked God for something *more*.

*"You've got to learn to get real with God He is okay with that."*

I remember stumbling once, and literally in the next moment, I went before God on my knees and said, "God, what I just did was in the full light of who You are and You know me through and through. I hate this thing that I'm doing, but I don't know how to break it. I need Your help." Three months after that prayer, on March 7, 2006, I had an encounter with the Holy Spirit.

## THE DAY I ENCOUNTERED THE HOLY SPIRIT

On that Tuesday in March, I was radically changed by the Holy Spirit. The encounter left me on my back with the power of God surging through me. You have to understand, I was a Bible-church kid, not a good charismatic boy who knew how to fall out in the Spirit. This was all new to me; nothing was fabricated. I was laying there with the power of God surging through my being, I was speaking in tongues, laughing and crying. At that exact moment, I was set free from the grip of pornography and never messed with it again.

There were two main effects that that encounter had on my life. One: I gained a power over sin that I didn't have before. The gospel that I previously knew gave me no permission to be completely free from it. I had a fresh understanding of the principle that the gospel promises us freedom from sin here and now, not just in the hereafter. Not only that, I had a fresh endowment of power to actually live that out. It's hard to argue with such fruit.

The second thing that happened was that I began to see the fruit and gifts of the Holy Spirit manifesting in my life in a dramatic, increased measure. My witnessing became bold. I had always felt growing up that I didn't have the power to witness or win souls. Suddenly, after being filled with the Spirit, I began to share Christ on a totally different level.

The impact of this baptism on my personal Christian life has been the most monumental shift I've experienced in my walk with Jesus. We can't afford to exempt ourselves from the blessed baptism in the Spirit. We've been baptized into the knowledge of forgiveness and sound doctrine, yet it's time to be baptized into the living Spirit of God. The biblical framework and model is painstakingly clear. Allow yourself to partake of the promise.

# 7

# ANSWERING COMMON MISCONCEPTIONS

As you might have gathered, I don't have a dog in the doctrinal fight. I am not a lifelong charismatic activist trying to gain new recruits. I personally don't gain from conservatives jumping ship. My ministry isn't predicated on filling a quota. I was a conservative evangelical who was radically changed by a genuine moment with the Holy Spirit. Not only that, but as I searched the scriptures, I saw a remarkably clear biblical framework for what I experienced.

Having said that, I'm well aware of many of the qualms over charismatic interests in the church. I'd like to breakdown a handful of the common misconceptions that have been aimed at those who renounce the modern practice of the baptism in the Holy Spirit. Not only that, I want to breakdown misconceptions about the baptism in the Spirit *within* the more Spirit-focused movement.

## MISCONCEPTION 1:
## IF YOU DON'T SPEAK IN TONGUES, YOU DON'T HAVE THE HOLY SPIRIT AND/OR YOU'RE NOT A CHRISTIAN.

Such a statement has no root in scripture whatsoever. Certain doctrines and ideas can be a challenge to refute because they contain a hint of the Word that's been manipulated to push an opinion. This, however, has no biblical framework. In fact Paul asked the question, "Do all speak in tongues?" (1 Corinthians 12:30) We see, continually, examples of believers who loved Jesus deeply, yet hadn't experienced the baptism in the Spirit or speaking in tongues. Apollos, as we've seen was saved, had the Holy Spirit in him, yet wasn't Spirit baptized. In fact, we see people who love Jesus, have been baptized in the Spirit, and haven't spoken with other tongues.

These sort of misguided ideas about the baptism of the Spirit come from an immature posture that divides over differences. "If you won't agree with me, then you aren't a brother to me" is sort of the school of thought, and it produces no health in the church. Questioning the salvation of those who think differently is actually a practice that takes place among the Word-camp just as much as it does among Spirit-camp who are pushing a belief.

Friends, this helps no one and only further separates the family of God. Let me be emphatically clear: *a Christian who doesn't speak in tongues is just as much a believer as anyone else who does.*

The "you're not a Christian if you don't speak in tongues" camp actually created a negative backlash among the opposing party. The backlash created a group that essentially said, "Sorry, but I have everything that I need, so I don't need any other additional experience, thank you very much.

The baptism in the Spirit isn't what you say it is." The result of these divisive ideas is two groups who alienate themselves even further from each other, instead of looking at the biblical model for what is sound and what is not.

I also want to make an important note, many have said that if you don't speak in tongues you don't have the Holy Spirit. The Holy Spirit indwells all believers at the moment of salvation. It's a mistake to believe otherwise when the Bible is clear that we are sealed with the Spirit the moment that we are born-again.

## MISCONCEPTION 2:
### THE SPIRIT CAMP OVER-EMPHASIZES

## *EXPERIENCE* AND *FEELING* WITH THE THINGS OF GOD.

Without question, there are wacky things that have taken place and do take place within the charismatic circle. If you hang around long enough, you'll see it. However, loopy doctrines and ideas are not in any way unique to the charismatic movement.

Odd practices and ideas are found in about every denomination, church, or movement on the planet. In fact, there are very mainstream movements that we all would recognize with unscriptural and strange tenants of faith.

A person misusing charismatic ideas and becoming flaky doesn't in any way steal from the legitimacy of the baptism in the Holy Spirit. The folks who showed up late to the upper room in Acts 2 certainly thought what they saw was strange.

In fact, they mocked those who experienced the baptism in the Spirit. Such things take place to this day. I also will say this: there are many world class and highly esteemed charismatic theologians and scholars.

> *"A person misusing charismatic ideas and becoming flaky doesn't in any way steal from the legitimacy of the baptism in the Holy Spirit."*

Perhaps there was a time when the pentecostal movement lacked representatives in the arena of biblical education and scholarship, but this isn't the case at all in our modern age. Sprit-focused Christianity is no longer a flaky, fringe movement. There are millions of balanced, level headed, Christ-loving people sprinkled throughout the earth who speak with other tongues and enjoy experiencing God.

Cantalamessa said something quite profound in this regard, "The most important fruit of the dialogue between the traditional churches and the Pentecostal churches will be achieving this aim: to recognize that Pentecost does not cast sacrament into a lesser role (especially the sacrament of baptism with water), and neither does sacrament cast Pentecost into a lesser position." (Come Creator Spirit p. 57)

## MISCONCEPTION 3:
## YOU HAVE TO QUALIFY YOURSELF TO BE WORTHY OF THE BAPTISM IN THE HOLY SPIRIT.

I referenced this topic earlier. The baptism in the Holy Spirit isn't a token blessing for those who have *graduated* into a position of worthiness. This has been taught in the past and is still taught in places. Besides teaching this verbally, this idea is also taught through attitude. Bad doctrine can be administered through an attitude. In this case, it's an attitude that sort of elevates the people who experience the baptism to a place that is only for God's elite. Good news: God's elite is every believer!

*We've already qualified for this experience through salvation. We've been made worthy of it through the blood.* We aren't wretched sinners trying to qualify for the baptism. Imagine if God joined Himself to a sinner in that way. That sinner would die immediately. The very fact that we remain living when God moves into us testifies of the cleanliness we've been given in Him.

To think that the Holy Spirit would inhabit our being at salvation, but somehow we must clean ourselves up for Him to baptize us is certainly misguided and unscriptural. Part of the work of the baptism in the Spirit is cleaning our actions so they match the cleanliness of our internal, born-again nature!

## MISCONCEPTION 4:
## THE BAPTISM IN THE HOLY SPIRIT ENDED WITH THE DEATH OF THE LAST APOSTLE.

This is a common sentiment regarding the baptism in the Spirit. It's an easy out to relegate such a powerful event to a past point in time. It exempts us from dealing with the sometimes uncomfortable and unpredictable side of Christianity. The problem is, it isn't found in the Bible.

As it's been said, if the early church needed the baptism of the Spirit to kick-start the gospel mission and spread the name of Jesus, how much more do we need it today? Why would they need something that we don't?

Peter preached the gospel to a group immediately following Pentecost and many were saved. He made a statement that I want to draw your attention to: "And Peter said to them, 'Repent and be baptized every one of you in the name of Jesus Christ for the forgiveness of your sins, and you will receive the gift of the Holy Spirit. For the promise is for you and for your children and for all who are far off, everyone whom the Lord our God calls to himself'" (Acts 2:38-39).

The phrase "for all who are far off" totally blew the top off of a generational conclusion to this powerful gift. We are living in the same dispensation that the church in Acts was. As a result, the same baptism in the Spirit is ever available and the scripture indicates no expiration date.

## MISCONCEPTION 5:
### YOU GET ALL OF THE HOLY SPIRIT WHEN YOU GET SAVED.

No doubt, the Holy Spirit indwells you at the

moment of salvation. This biblical fact does not, however, negate the *possibility* of a subsequent experience of the baptism in the Spirit that the scriptures profusely demonstrate.

In John 14, Jesus spoke of the Spirit to His disciples, "You know Him, for He dwells with you and will be in you" (John 14:17). Obviously, the disciples couldn't receive the indwelling Holy Spirit because they weren't yet born again, because Christ hadn't risen from the dead — providing a sufficient sacrifice. When He did rise from the dead, they had their born again experience in John 20 when He appeared to them and breathed the Holy Spirit into them.

Not only did Jesus speak of the *indwelling* of the Holy Spirit by being saved, but also the baptism of the Holy Spirit that was to come. He related at the end of Luke's gospel, "And behold, I am sending the promise of my Father upon you. But stay in the city until you are clothed with power from on high" (Luke 24:49).

Clearly Christ was distinguishing between his redemptive work on the cross that would prepare them to *receive the Holy Spirit* as a seal of redemption (Eph. 1:13) and the subsequent experience where Jesus would baptize them in the Holy Spirit on Pentecost. If the disciples received all that they needed when they were saved, the book of Acts would have bypassed the upper room and simply began recording the works of the early church. Yet the scriptures actually take us to the necessary experience of the baptism in the Spirit.

The Word described the coming of the Holy Spirit like this: "And suddenly there came from heaven a sound like a mighty rushing wind, and it filled the entire house where they were sitting" (Acts 2:2). I find it fascinating that when they were born again, the coming of the Spirit was described as a breath. When they were baptized in the Spirit, it was described as a wind.

The Greek word *baptized* is the word *baptizo*. This word was used to describe dipping a cloth into dye. In biblical times, the people would dip a cloth into dye to color it. When the cloth was completely immersed, they would pull the cloth out and you couldn't tell where the cloth ended and where the dye began. This is the picture of being baptized in the Spirit. It's being so completely immersed in God that you cannot tell where you begin and where God starts. It's a co-laboring in which you are clothed with God Himself… colored by His character and nature.

# 8

## AN INVITATION FOR MORE

It would only be fitting at this point to give you an invitation to be baptized with the Holy Spirit. My heart is not just explanation through books and reading, but demonstration through a vibrant encounter with the Holy Spirit of God.

God is jealous for you. The Spirit baptism is an act of the jealousy of God, enduing every ounce of your being with power. God isn't reluctant in giving His gifts, but ever available to give with liberality. The only prerequisite to being baptized in the Spirit is to be born again through faith in Jesus and to simply **ask** for it.

If you don't understand the power of the blood, you will try to work for this free gift. Know this: you're spotless before God and worthy of this experience in the sight of God. He sees you so far separated from sin that you and sin are strangers as far as God is concerned. Now, simply ask and receive.

> "And I tell you, ask, and it will be given to you; seek, and you will find; knock, and it will be opened to you. For everyone who asks receives, and the one who seeks finds, and to the one who knocks it will be opened.
>
> What father among you, if his son asks for a fish, will instead of a fish give him a serpent; or if he asks for an egg, will give him a scorpion? If you then, who are evil, know how to give good gifts to your children, how much more will the heavenly Father give the Holy Spirit to those who ask him!" (Luke 11:9-13)

And again in the 14th chapter of John's Gospel Jesus says, "I will ask the Father, and He will give you another Helper, that He may be with you forever; *that is* the Spirit of truth, whom the world cannot receive, because it does not see Him or know Him, *but* you know Him because He abides with you and will be in you." (John 14:16-17)

We see from this Scripture that Jesus is the *asker*, the Father is the *giver* and that makes us the *receiver*! How confident should we be in receiving the Holy Spirit, if

Jesus is the one asking the Father on our behalf, and He assures us that the Father will give Him what He asks!

> "Those who want it prepare themselves, not only by confessing and repenting sincerely of their sins, but also by taking part in meetings where they receive teaching and where they come into a living and joyous contact with the great truths and realities of the faith: the love of God, sin, salvation, new life, transformation in Christ, charisms, and the fruits of the Spirit. And all of this is an atmosphere marked chiefly by a profound sense of belonging and being loved and cared for."
> —Cantalamessa (Come Creator Spirit, p. 54)

As you meditate on these truths and passages, let the Lord encounter you as you encounter Him. If you feel sounds and words in another language rising up in your spirit, began to release the utterance of that heavenly language. If the Lord moves you to tears, embrace the weeping. If you're lifted up in laughter, let it happen. Be filled and continually flooded with Him.

You can't always predict just what you'll experience in this place. In the book "New Covenant" the author describes, "I was in an aeroplane, on a journey, and I was reading the last chapter of a book on the Holy Spirit. Suddenly it was as if the Spirit came out of the page and entered into my body. Tears began to stream from my eyes. I began to pray. I was overcome by a Power much greater than I." —In "New Covenant" (Ann Arbor, Mich. June 1984, p.12)

Though experiences like this are common and are often associated with being baptized in the Spirit, I want to make it clear that a believer should not think twice if nothing seems to happen right away.

Just as the disciples were encouraged to wait for the promise of the Holy Spirit, you too may have to wait. Don't despair and don't lose heart. If nothing happens immediately, don't question your salvation or your own worthiness. Instead, go back to the Scriptures and encourage yourself that the promise of being baptized in the Holy Spirit is just that, a promise from your heavenly Father. So rest in the strength of His promise, ask for Him to baptize you in the Holy Spirit and wait with expectancy in your heart as you receive this priceless gift. Your approach and waiting is never without a corresponding action from God.

It is worth reiterating in this section that if you have put your faith in Jesus, his death, burial and resurrection, then you have been born again and sealed with the promised Holy Spirit (Eph. 1:13). So it is with confidence and expectation that regardless of whether or not you can point to a specific experience where God gave you power, you can be sure that your Father in heaven will continue to bring all of the subsequent glories (1 Peter 1:11) of the Gospel into your life.

Thomas Aquinas writes, "There is an invisible sending of the Holy Spirit every time any progress in virtue or increase in grace takes place...when someone enters upon a new activity or into a new state of grace: for example when a person receives the grace to work miracles, or the gift of prophecy, or when spurred by the fervor of love a person risks martyrdom or gives up possessions or undertakes some difficult or exacting task." —Summa Theologiae I (q. 43 a. 6 ad 2) Rest in the assurance of this *invisible sending* as you progress and increase.

March 7, 2006, wasn't my last encounter with the Holy Spirit. The initial baptism in the Spirit is not the climax that then leads to a resolution and an ending. No, the baptism of the Spirit is a continual climax available as you run the course of the entirety of your Christian life.

"The most common result of this grace is that the Holy Spirit, who before was the more-or-less abstract object of a person's intellectual assent of faith, becomes a fact of experience, as we have seen that of the Spirit's very nature the Spirit should always be. A well-known theologian has written:

> 'We cannot doubt that in this life we can experience

grace in such a way that it gives us a sense of freedom and opens up horizons that are entirely new, making a profound impression on us, transforming us and moulding in us, even over a long period of time, a more inward Christian attitude. There is nothing that prevents us calling that kind of experience a baptism in the Spirit.'"

—Cantalamessa, (Come Creator Spirit, p. 55)

This is the life that we are commissioned *into*. Like Cantalamessa stated, a life in which the Spirit and the Word come together creating perfect synergy *opens our horizons*, installs freedom, and transforms us into the image of Christ. These realities aren't mere perks of the Christian life but the very foundation of it.

ABOUT THE AUTHOR

Peter K. Louis and his wife Kristi live in Dallas Texas with their four children. He is the founder of Braveheart Ministries, a Gospel-focused ministry aimed at equipping the Body of Christ to walk in love and to grow up into all the fullness of Christ. Peter enjoys golf, fishing and hunting and one day dreams of playing a round at Augusta National.

FOR MORE INFORMATION ON **PETER LOUIS** AND **BRAVEHEART MINISTRIES** VISIT:

**BRAVEHEARTMINISTRIES.ORG**

Made in the USA
Las Vegas, NV
15 July 2021